BL: 5.5
ARPTS: 0.5

101 Facts About

SNAKES

Julia Barnes

Gareth Stevens Publishing
A WORLD ALMANAC EDUCATION GROUP COMPANY

Please visit our web site at: www.garethstevens.com
For a free color catalog describing Gareth Stevens Publishing's
list of high-quality books and multimedia programs,
call 1-800-542-2595 (USA) or 1-800-387-3178 (Canada).
Gareth Stevens Publishing's fax: (414) 332-3567.

Library of Congress Cataloging-in-Publication Data

Barnes, Julia, 1955-
    101 facts about snakes / by Julia Barnes. — North American ed.
       p. cm. — (101 facts about predators)
    Includes bibliographical references and index.
    Summary: Presents information about different kinds of snakes.
    ISBN 0-8368-4040-2 (lib. bdg.)
    1. Snakes—Miscellanea—Juvenile literature. [1. Snakes—Miscellanea.]
  I. Title: One hundred one facts about snakes. II. Title: One hundred
and one facts about snakes. III. Title.
  QL666.O6B325   2004
  597.96—dc22   2003059174

This North American edition first published in 2004 by
Gareth Stevens Publishing
A World Almanac Education Group Company
330 West Olive Street, Suite 100
Milwaukee, WI 53212 USA

This U.S. edition copyright © 2004 by Gareth Stevens, Inc. Original edition © 2003 by First
Stone Publishing. First published in 2003 by First Stone Publishing, 4/5 The Marina,
Harbour Road, Lydney, Gloucestershire, GL15 5ET, United Kingdom. Additional end matter
© 2004 by Gareth Stevens, Inc.

First Stone Series Editor: Claire Horton-Bussey
First Stone Designer: Sarah Williams
Geographical consultant: Miles Ellison
Gareth Stevens Editor: Catherine Gardner

Printed in Hong Kong through Printworks Int. Ltd.

1 2 3 4 5 6 7 8 9 08 07 06 05 04

WHAT IS A PREDATOR?

Predators are nature's hunters – the creatures that must kill in order to survive. They come in all shapes and sizes, ranging from the mighty lion to the slithering snake.

Although predators are different in many ways, they do have some things in common. All predators are necessary in the balance of nature. Predators keep the number of other animals in control, which prevents starvation and disease. In addition, all predators adapted, or changed, to survive where they live. They developed special skills to find **prey** and kill it in the quickest, simplest way possible.

In many parts of the world, the snake, which does not hear or see as well as many other animals, is the most feared predator. It hides in the most unlikely places and glides in silently to make its kill.

Arctic Ocean

North
Pacific
Ocean

NORTH
AMERICA

North
Atlantic
Ocean

SOUTH
AMERICA

South
Atlantic
Ocean

Key

Ice: Where land is covered by ice. *No snakes are found in this area.*

Tundra: Close to the arctic circle, this cold region experiences one to three months per year when the average monthly temperature rises above freezing. *No snakes are found in this area.*

Temperate: A region where there are mild/warm summers (50-68° F/ 10-20° C) and cool winters (36-68° F/2-minus 20° C). *grass snake, adder, milk snake.*

Tropical: Hot areas where there are no seasonal variations. *giant green anaconda, boa constrictor.*

Desert: Dry places where very little water is available. *sand boa, rattlesnake.*

Mediterranean: A region where there are warm to hot summers (over 68° F/ 20° C) and mild winters (43° F/6° C or higher). *horseshoe whip snake, leopard snake.*

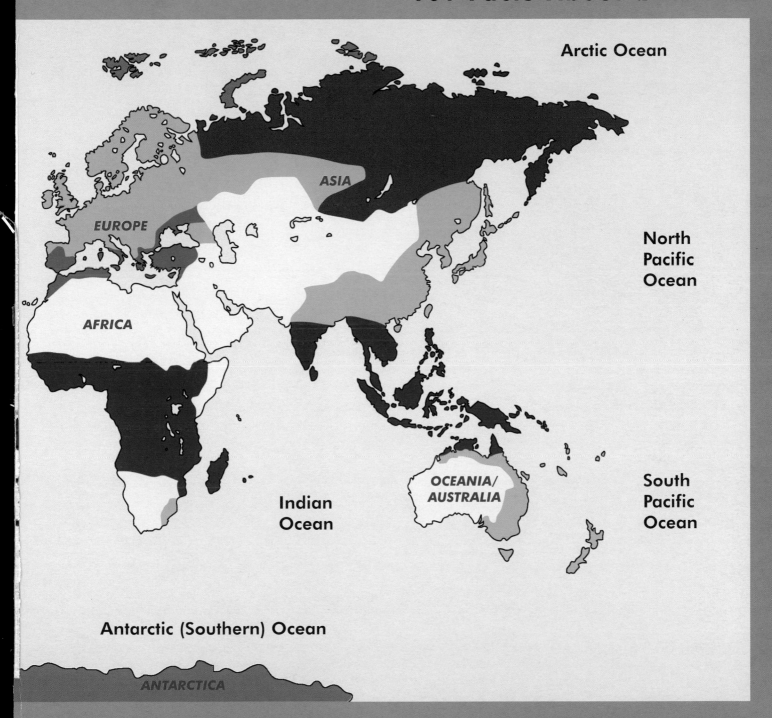

Arctic Ocean

ASIA

EUROPE

North
Pacific
Ocean

AFRICA

Indian
Ocean

OCEANIA/
AUSTRALIA

South
Pacific
Ocean

Antarctic (Southern) Ocean

ANTARCTICA

3 **Terrestrial** snakes live mainly on the ground. **Arboreal** snakes, such as the long-nosed tree snake (right) of southeast Asia, spend most of their time living in trees.

1 About 2,700 **species** of snakes are alive today. Snakes survive in all but the coldest parts of the world.

2 Snakes live in deserts (above), rain forests, grasslands, marshes (right), and swamps. Some snake species make their homes only in the sea.

4 In fact, every continent on Earth – except the frozen ground of Antarctica (see pages 4-5) – has some species of snakes.

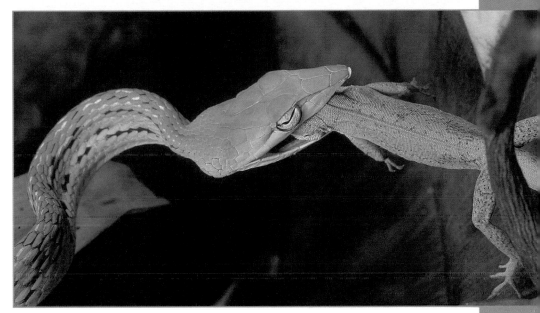

5 Some islands, such as New Zealand, Hawaii, Iceland, Ireland, and Newfoundland, do not have snakes living in the wild.

6 A **legend** says that St. Patrick drove all of the snakes out of Ireland when he brought Christianity there in the fifth century. It is more likely that snakes never lived there.

7 Less than a quarter of all snake species are **venomous**, and only a few of the venomous species are a real danger to people.

8 Today's snakes trace their **ancestors** back to animals that lived about 150 million years ago, in the days when dinosaurs roamed the land.

7

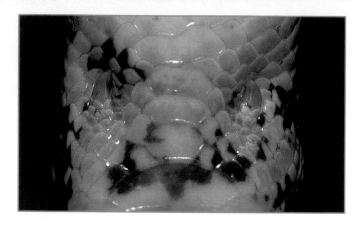

9 Snakes developed from lizards that were able to burrow through loose sand or move in thick **vegetation** more easily without legs to get in the way.

10 Some snakes, such as boa constrictors from South America, have traces of back legs that form two tiny spurs on their bodies (above).

11 Snakes, like all other **reptiles**, are cold-blooded. They are not able to make their own body heat.

12 All snakes have the same basic shape, but their sizes vary greatly.

13 The longest snake is the reticulated python (above right) that lives in rain forests of southeastern Asia. It can grow to be about 30 feet (9 meters), which equals the height of a three-story house.

14 Some kinds of blind snakes (right) are

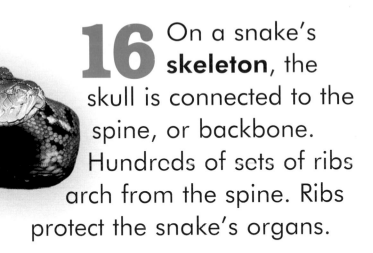

16 On a snake's **skeleton**, the skull is connected to the spine, or backbone. Hundreds of sets of ribs arch from the spine. Ribs protect the snake's organs.

only about the size of earthworms. They grow to be no more than 4 inches (10 centimeters) long.

15 Green anacondas, which live in South America, set weight records for snakes. These giants can tip the scale at 550 pounds (250 kilograms)!

17 The snake's organs, such as its heart and lungs, are long and thin to fit into the snake's narrow and cylinder-shaped body.

18 Most snakes have a long, thin right lung and a tiny left lung that does little, if any, breathing.

19 Most species of sea snakes (below) have one large lung. Sea snakes can stay under the water for several hours.

20 When a sea snake swims, it can close its nostrils to keep out water. The sea snake breathes air by swimming to the surface of the water.

21 A snake's stomach is long and stretchy. Many kinds of snakes eat a huge meal and then rest for many weeks, or even months, before they need to eat again.

22 Most snakes move slowly, but the black mamba

of Africa can travel 12 miles (19 kilometers) per hour in short bursts.

23 Only some snakes spend most of their time slithering over the land. Others climb trees (right) or swim in water. Snakes move to match their **habitat**.

24 Most snakes wriggle from side to side in S-shaped bends. The larger snakes, such as the Burmese python from southeast Asia, use strong muscles to pull themselves straight ahead in the style of a caterpillar.

25 Some snakes, such as the green whip snake from North America, move in an accordion style. They climb or glide by first stretching their bodies and then pulling them together.

26 Moving in the loose and hot sand of the desert, snakes use a quick, sideways motion, which is called sidewinding (below).

27 When swimming, a sea snake pushes against the water and arches in S-shaped bends. The sea snake's head is flat on both sides, which gives the snake extra power in the water.

28 Golden tree snakes of southeastern Asia and other snakes that live in trees look like they fly. Really, they drop from one branch and glide to the next one.

29 While a tree snake glides through the air, large, S-shaped waves pass along its body. It twists its tail to keep its balance.

30 A cobra seems to dance to the music

skin can feel the **vibrations** that some sounds make in the ground.

played by a snake charmer (above). The movement of the instrument, not its music, attracts the snake.

32 Snakes never blink, and their eyelids do not move to close their eyes. Instead of upper and lower eyelids, a **transparent** cap, called a spectacle, protects each eye (below).

31 Snakes do not have ears on their heads. They cannot hear sound that travels in the air, such as a snake charmer's pipe or the rattle of another snake. Their

33 While some species of snakes are nearly blind, others notice even tiny movements of possible **prey**.

34 Snakes that hunt in the daylight, such as one of the garter snakes from North and Central America (below), see more clearly than other snakes.

35 The forked tongue of a snake helps it feel things in its path. Also, its tongue, together with its keen nose, gives the snake its important sense of smell.

36 As a snake flicks its tongue in and out of its mouth, it presses the tips to the **Jacobson's organ** on the roof of its mouth.

37 The snake uses its Jacobson's organ to sort out all of the odors in its habitat. Its sensitive sense of smell helps the snake hunt its prey, stay away from danger, and find mates for breeding.

38 Many people who have never touched

a snake think its skin might feel cold and slimy. In fact, a snake's skin feels warm, dry, and smooth.

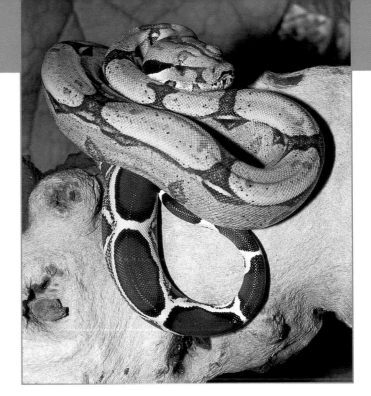

39 From head to tail, snakes are covered by **scales**. The overlapping rows of scales form a tough covering that protects snakes from bumps and scrapes.

40 Humans shed little flakes of old skin and grow new skin all of the time. Snakes shed worn-out skin all at once. After the old skin falls away, snakes have bright, new skin (above).

41 Snakes may shed, or **slough**, many times a year. The number of times a snake sloughs depends on its age and species.

42 Venomous snakes often have brightly colored skin. Bright colors warn predators to stay away.

45 Tree snakes usually have skin in green or brown colors to match the leaves and bark of the tree.

43 Some types of milk snakes that live in the southeastern part of the United States appear to be venomous (above). The red, yellow, and black bands of color make them look like venomous types of snakes, so predators stay away.

46 Snakes that live in deserts, such as a sand boa (below), are the yellows and browns of the desert landscape.

47 Good camouflage not only protects a snake from its predators but

44 Many snakes have skin that blends in with their surroundings. This is known as **camouflage**.

also helps it hunt. The snake blends into its habitat while it waits for its prey.

48 The type of food a snake eats depends on what is available. Most snakes eat rats, mice, voles, and lizards.

49 Green anacondas lurk in marshlands and swamps. They patiently wait for birds, turtles, and caimans, which are related to crocodiles.

50 It takes a special trick for the African egg-eating snake (above) to enjoy its meal. It swallows an egg whole and then uses its pointed backbones to crack open the egg. The snake can swallow the soft yolk, but it must spit out the hard pieces of the eggshell.

51 The northern water snake from North America lives in freshwater and eats a diet of fish, frogs, salamanders, and toads.

54 Fewer snake species actively search out prey. The smaller, faster kinds of snakes prowl for eggs or baby animals in nests.

55 Pythons and boas (left) have special heat sensors on their faces or lips that help them find prey in the dark.

56 Different snakes have different ways of killing their prey. The

52 The California king snake of the United States is among the snake species that eat other kinds of snakes. King snakes eat the venomous rattlesnakes.

53 To hunt, most snakes lie still and wait (right) until an animal comes close.

American racer swallows a whole lizard or frog while it is still alive.

57 In other species, the snake kills its prey first, before it tries to swallow the meal.

58 Anacondas and boas kill their prey before they eat. Called **constrictors**, they use their strong bodies to **suffocate** their victims.

59 Constrictors kill by coiling themselves around their prey and tightly squeezing (right).

60 Venomous snakes kill prey with large teeth called fangs. In some snakes, the fangs are in the front of the mouth. In others, the fangs are in the back.

61 Fangs let the snake put venom, which is a poisonous liquid, into the prey animal.

64 Cobras and coral snakes, along with sea snakes, have short fangs in the front of their mouths. Venom flows down the fangs as the snake bites.

62 Sharp teeth line the jaws of a snake. It does not need teeth to chew food into small pieces. The teeth point backward and help the snake grip its prey.

65 Vipers have fangs in front, too (left). Their fangs can move. The fangs stay folded on the roof of the mouth when they are not in use but can swing forward as the snake bites.

63 A snake sometimes breaks a tooth, but it is able to grow new teeth during its whole life.

66 The world's longest venomous snake is the king cobra, which grows as long as 18 feet (5.5 m).

67 A king cobra has enough venom to kill an elephant.

68 The black mamba (below) has a fatal bite. Its venom kills a human in twenty minutes.

69 The snakes with the most deadly venom live in the sea. The venom of a marine cobra is one hundred times stronger than the venom of a cobra that lives on land.

70 A snake-bite victim (above) gets a kind of medicine called antivenin. Making an antivenin starts by **milking** a snake for a supply of its venom.

71 The snake has the amazing ability to swallow its prey whole.

72 After a snake grabs its prey, it spreads the two sides of its lower jaw and stretches its mouth wide enough to hold the animal.

73 Snakes can handle some big meals. An African rock python (above) can swallow a 132-pound (60-kg) impala, which is a kind of antelope.

74 Slowly, a snake pulls its prey into its body. Swallowing a big animal can take a long time. The snake has a special breathing tube that allows the snake to take in air when its mouth is full.

75 When it is time to breed, male snakes follow the scent trails left by female snakes.

76 Some snakes, such as rattlesnakes and adders, fight over females. They wrestle with each other to find out which of them is the strongest.

77 A male and female snake may stay together for the breeding season (right), but soon after breeding, they go their separate ways.

78 Snakes such as rat snakes, milk snakes, cobras, and pythons lay eggs to produce young.

79 A few weeks after **mating**, the female finds a safe place to lay her eggs. She may bury them in sandy soil or hide them under a rock or a log.

80 The king cobra is the only snake that builds a special nest for its eggs and stays to incubate, or warm, the eggs.

81 Most female snakes can lay between six and thirty eggs, but some lay about one hundred eggs.

82 Female king cobras stay at the nest to guard their eggs from harm. Most snakes leave after they lay their eggs.

83 The eggs hatch in two to four months, and tiny snakes come out of the shells (below).

86 All the eggs hatch inside the female, which gives birth to as many as fifty young snakes.

87 After the snakes are born, most mothers leave the babies, which must learn to survive on their own.

84 Snakes such as the rattlesnake (above), garter snake, adder, boa, and sea snake (right) give birth to live young.

85 Snakes that have live young start life as eggs. The eggs develop inside the female's body instead of on land.

88 In warm climates, snakes are born at any time of the year. In other places, they are born when food is most available.

89 The small newborns (below) are not able to kill or eat big prey. They do, however, catch bite-size snacks of flies, worms, and other insects.

90 Most snakes grow quickly. They might double or triple their length during their first year of life.

91 To make room for their fast-growing bodies, young snakes shed their skin more often than adults of the same species.

92 Big or small, snakes are predators. They hunt live prey. Some snakes, however, are prey, too. They are eaten by other animals.

93 The snake hunters include mongooses (above), crocodiles, eagles, and foxes. Predators keep a special lookout for young snakes, which are easier to catch than older ones.

94 To stay safe from predators, snakes use their skin coloring as camouflage to blend in with their habitat (below). Using camouflage is just one of the many ways snakes stay away from danger.

95 Members of the cobra family, which live in both Africa and Asia, rely on their hoods to make themselves look big and scare away predators.

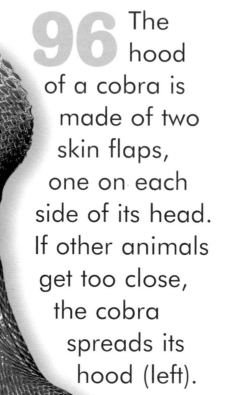

96 The hood of a cobra is made of two skin flaps, one on each side of its head. If other animals get too close, the cobra spreads its hood (left).

97 A spitting cobra spits venom into the eyes of an attacker from a distance of as much as 6.5 feet (2 m).

98 If the cottonmouth snake is attacked, it swishes its tail at its enemy, giving off a spray that smells so bad predators run away.

99 A western hognose snake, which can be found in some parts of the United States, fools its enemies by playing dead (top left). The snake rolls on its back, lets its mouth hang open, and lies completely still.

101 From the gigantic king cobra to the small garter snake (below), snakes should be respected by humans. These predators play an important role in the balance of nature.

100 Of all predators, snakes may be the most feared and hated by humans. In some places, people try to kill all of the snakes.

Glossary

ancestors: early relatives.

arboreal: tree-dwelling.

camouflage: coloring that blends in with the surroundings.

constrictors: snakes that kill their prey by squeezing their coils around its body.

habitat: the place where an animal naturally lives and grows.

Jacobson's organ: a sensing center in the roof of a snake's mouth that helps it detect odors.

legend: a story handed down from the past.

mating: pairing of male and female in order to reproduce.

milking: taking venom from snakes.

predators: animals that kill other animals for food.

prey: the animal a predator chooses to hunt and kill.

reptiles: cold-blooded animals that breathe air and have no legs or short legs, such as lizards, turtles, alligators, and snakes.

scales: horny plates that protect the snake's skin.

skeleton: the bones of an animal.

slough: to shed skin.

species: types of animals or plants that are alike in many ways.

suffocate: to prevent breathing.

terrestrial: ground-dwelling.

transparent: see-through.

vegetation: plants and shrubs.

venomous: having poison.

vibrations: the movements in a solid surface made by sound.

More Books to Read

All About Your Snake
Chris Newman
(Barrons)

The Giant Book of Snakes and Slithery Creatures
Jim Pipe (Millbrook)

Snakes (Our Wild World series)
Deborah Dennard
(Creative Publishing)

Snakes, Salamanders and Lizards
Diane Burns
(NorthWord Press)

Web Sites

American International Rattlesnake Museum
www.rattlesnakes.com/core.html

Pet Reptiles
www.petreptiles.com/Snake/
snake-pet.php3

Singapore Zoological Society
www.szgdocent.org/cc/
c-record.htm

Snakes and Reptiles
www.snakesandreptiles.com/
snake_care.html

To find additional web sites, use a reliable search engine to find one or more of the following keywords: **constrictors**, **snakes**, **venomous**.

Index